When the Ground Beneath You Shifts

THE MIGHTY MOUNTAIN

KIWITTA PASCHAL

THE MIGHTY MOUNTAIN

When the Ground Beneath you Shifts

Kiwitta Paschal

Blkpawn Publishing

Copyright ©2026 Kiwitta Paschal

All rights reserved. No part of this publication may be reproduced, distributed, or transmitted in any form or by any means, including photocopying, recording, or other electronic or mechanical methods, without the prior written permission of the publisher, except as permitted by U.S. copyright law. To request permissions, contact the publisher at legal@blkpawnpublishing.com

Paperback: ISBN 979-8-9915273-2-3
Ebook: 979-8-9915273-3-0

Library of Congress Number: 2025926200

First paperback edition March 2026

Cover designed by Getcovers

Edited by Becky Ross Michael

Published by Blkpawn Publishing
www.blkpawnpublishing.com

'But if we look forward to something we don't yet have, we must wait patiently and confidently.'

Romans 8:25

Table of Contents

Title 1

Front Matter 3

Introduction 9

Part I – The Revelation 13

    Chapter 1 - Saturday Grocery Run 15

    Chapter 2 – Robert & Kim's Ride to Small Group 22

    Chapter 3 –Joe & Linda's Ride to Small Group 28

    Chapter 4 – The Arrival 36

Part II – The Rupture 45

    Chapter 5 – Now That Everyone's Here 47

    Chapter 6 – We're All Ears 53

    Chapter 7 – Can't Hold It in Anymore 64

    Chapter 8 - The Mighty Mountain 69

Part III – The Refinement & Redemption 75

    Chapter 9 - Who Is in the Center? 77

    Chapter 10 - What's Big For Some Is Small For Others 84

    Chapter 11 - We Can Be the Stones 89

Afterward 98
Acknowledgements 102
Continue the Journey 104

Introduction

Before you step into this book, let me give you a quick heads-up about what you're about to read. This isn't a "how-to" book with neat lists, quick steps, or bullet points to check off. It's not written in the traditional teaching style. Instead, it unfolds as a story inside a story. This is a tale about ordinary people navigating real-life struggles. Within their conversations, a parable called "The Mighty Mountain" is revealed, holding lessons about faith, purpose, and change.

Why tell it this way? Because life rarely comes to us in neatly packaged points. It comes through conversations at the dinner table, through quiet prayers, through stories passed down that suddenly impact us differently when we're in the middle of a storm. That's the rhythm of this book: everyday life mixed with eternal truth.

So, let me introduce you to the circle you'll be joining. At the center are Sean and Dani, the leaders of their small group. They are the next couple to host the monthly gathering of friends from church to go through a topical book or sermon series. Small groups are places where people open their homes, cook meals, and create inviting spaces for real conversations that often go deeper than answering discussion prompts, small talk, and sports banter. You could say they *do* life together in those spaces. Around the table sit Joe and Linda, married for fifteen years, juggling careers, life with a child, and the possibility of a big family transition. There's also Robert and Kim, newlyweds compared to the others, navigating the weight of family responsibilities while balancing dreams for the future. The story opens with Sean and Dani in the throes of life, leaving their preteen son at home for the first time, when they run into a couple from their small group in a grocery store.

These aren't perfect people. They carry worry, doubt, fear, and hard questions just like you and me. At times, they laugh. At other times, they fight tears. But what binds them together is more than friendship; it's faith and a willingness to show up for each other in the middle of life's changes.

When they gather, stories surface. Secrets slip out between bites of lasagna. Questions about identity, purpose, and God's plan hang in the air. It's in these conversations that Sean shares an old parable passed down to him by his mother: the story of "The Mighty Mountain." That's the heartbeat of this book.

The story isn't about geology or weather. It's about us. It's about identity, loss, and the painful ways life sometimes breaks us down. But it's also about how God can use what looks like failure or ruin to position us for a greater purpose.

I encourage you not to rush past the conversations. Don't dismiss the parable as inessential or overly simple. Let the imagery breathe. Sit with the characters as they wrestle with making sense of it all, because you'll likely also wrestle with whatever life throws at you. That's the point.

Most importantly, know this: while the story explores heavy themes, such as career loss, illness, relocation, and disappointment, it's not written to weigh you down. It's written to give you hope. There's humor here, joy here, friendship here. And above all, there's the reminder that God is with us through it all.

So, as you turn the page, don't worry about figuring out every detail. Just walk with these characters. Listen to their questions. Let the parable settle in your heart. You might not see its full meaning right away, and that's okay. Truth has a way of unfolding over time.

Take a deep breath. Pull up a chair at the table. And let's step into the story together.

Part I - The Revelation

Chapter 1 - Saturday Grocery Run

"Sean, what else is on the shopping list?" Dani asked. Her brown eyes gazed upon her husband's bald head.

"Ah, I think we have everything for the week. I hope we have enough food and snacks for this growing eleven-year-old with a tapeworm at home," Sean joked.

Rolling her eyes and shaking her head, Dani wasn't amused. "We need to hurry; I'm still not fully comfortable leaving him at home alone."

"Don't worry. It's only been a little over an hour. Mel will be fine. I'm sure he's in his room playing video games." Sean failed to find a sign of assurance as he searched Dani's face.

Taking a step towards the registers, he overheard a strong northeastern accent. "Hey, Sean, Dani. We didn't expect to see you here!" said Joe.

"Hey, what's going on, buddy? Are you here alone?" Sean said.

"No, there's my friend," said Dani with a big smile as Linda walked around the corner. "Linda, I love what you did with your hair; the highlights really complement your eyes. The length looks a little shorter. Did you cut it?"

"They just trimmed the ends," said Linda. "I prefer my hair shoulder length. It's so much more manageable with my busy schedule." Pushing up on her wavy curls, Linda continued. "There was a time I would have made the leap to wear a short, amazing, cropped style like you. But like I said, I'm constantly chasing time, trying to figure out where it went."

The compliment made Dani momentarily forget about Mel back home. Grinning, she admitted, "It's not as difficult as you might imagine."

Joe's short, stocky frame fit the cart perfectly. He leaned on the handle of the empty shopping basket. "Sean, have you been watching the playoffs?"

"Man, they've been great," said Sean. "I didn't think Atlanta was going to come back the way they did. I was surprised!"

"Friends, we have to head back home," said Dani. "Mel's by himself for the first time, and I'm a nervous wreck. Sean is unfazed. Linda, you must tell me the secret for staying calm."

Sean received the cue and took a step towards the front of the store.

Linda's shoulders drooped slightly. Dani's concern for Mel distracted her from her real talent for reading the room. Any other time, she would have sensed an issue and would have drawn it out of Linda, just as a skilled nurse would take blood. Linda was secretly hoping, as well, that Dani would sense an issue but couldn't bring herself to say something.

Not letting the moment pass, Joe asked, "Before you go, when are we getting together again?"

Twisting his body around, Sean's warm tenor voice responded. "You're right! We meet monthly, and it's been about three weeks since we last met. We met at Robert and Kim's house last, so that means Dani and I are next." He glanced into his wife's eyes for confirmation.

"Sure," Dani hastily responded. "I think our calendar is clear for this Saturday. I'll send out a text message to the group chat to confirm."

"Great, we're looking forward to it!" said Joe. "There are some things Linda and I want to talk about with you both."

No one noticed the beads of sweat collecting on top of Joe's thinning hairline. He did feel the back of his neck get red hot from the laser beams Linda was shooting out of her eyes. She thought to herself, *This wasn't the plan. This isn't how it was supposed to happen.* Only Joe recognized how uneasy his wife was, but he knew he had to say something and not let the moment slip by. Underneath the polished and robust exterior forged by years in Corporate America lay an anxious woman troubled by a secret known only to her husband.

"Sounds good," said Sean. "Enjoy the rest of your week!"

Sean extended his hand to shake and pulled Joe in for the one-armed man-hug. Dani hugged Linda and air kissed her. Sean hugged Linda from the side as Dani raised her hand to wave at Joe. Sean and Dani proceeded to the checkout to pay for their groceries and head home.

When Sean and Dani reached the end of the aisle and turned the corner, Linda broke character. "Why did you say that?" she asked.

The sweat on Joe's head didn't stop forming. "What? All I said was 'we want to talk to you about something.'"

"That's not how I wanted to announce the news, Joe."

"Linda, sweetie, I understand, but we have a lot to juggle. We haven't mentioned anything to Joey; we aren't even sure how he's going to take the news. Things are moving fast, and I'm sensing we're on uneasy ground." Joe grabbed Linda's hands, looked into her eyes, and calmly stated, "I love spending time with Sean and Dani. There's a sense of peace around them. Whenever we get together, I'm always learning something new. I know Sean has some wisdom to share with us. I can feel it."

"My mind is racing 1000 miles per hour," said Linda. "But I trust you. Who knew after 15 years of marriage we'd be contemplating changes like this? I love the life we've built up and the friends we have here in College Park. I'm worried about how this news will affect everything we have."

Joe wrapped his arms around Linda and pulled her close. Linda dropped her head and nuzzled her face on the side of his neck, resting her head on his shoulder.

"I love you, Joe."

"I love you too, sweetie."

Chapter 2 - Robert & Kim's Ride to Small Group

Normally, the radio would be on. Kim would be singing the lyrics as Robert happily drove his new bride wherever she wanted to go. But this time, the ride to Sean and Dani's house was eerily quiet.

Breaking the silence, Kim said, "Look, babe, I know you didn't want to leave your family back at your parents' house, but I think that we had to step away for a few hours to process everything."

"Are you sure? I don't think it was the right thing to do. I feel awful for leaving Mom and my sister back home with Dad."

"I'm sure," Kim said confidently. "You didn't hear me in the other room because you were watching over your dad, but I was talking with your mom and Cheryl. Your mom definitely understood how seeing your dad in that fragile state affected you. She was worried about what was going on in your head. I shared that we had prior plans to meet with our friends but would gladly cancel to figure out what we need to do."

"Okay, and?"

"And, like I said, she was worried about her son and wanted to help calm him down. You know your mom, 'I can't have two of my babies sick,'" Kim parroted, trying to ease the tension. "I don't have kids yet, but I can empathize with her and all of you, frankly. So, we agreed that you and I would go to dinner and would head back to the house in a few hours."

"And just leave them to watch Dad?" Robert questioned in disbelief.

"Yes. I was surprised, too, when they said it. But Cheryl explained this wasn't the first time he wandered off. Last year, he began misplacing things around the house and calling people the wrong names. Apparently, a few months ago, she caught Dad walking out the door, confused about where he was going. About an hour later, he was fine again and shrugged it off as just being tired."

"What? Are you kidding me?"

"Babe, I know. I'm just as shocked. They told me this is the third time it's happened. Looking back, the signs were there, but no one wanted to admit it."

The revelation hit Robert hard, and his head dropped momentarily before he looked up at the red light.

"Kim, I don't know how I could have been so oblivious to it, but this time was serious! He wandered into the next town over. Nobody told me? Nobody warned me that he was showing early signs of dementia? Not a heads up or anything? If something had happened, I don't think I could have forgiven myself." Tears welled up and streamed down Robert's face.

Kim reached into her large tote bag and grabbed a tissue. She leaned on the console of the large SUV, reached across his face, and wiped Robert's tears.

"I don't know if we should bring it up with the group," Robert stated.

"Why not? I think we can trust everyone. Dani and Sean are amazing. You have your sister to look up to, but I'm an only child. So, I view Dani and Sean like my older brother and sister. You, your parents, and Cheryl are *my* family. I'm not as close with my mom as I am with your family. When my parents divorced, I chose to be with my dad. When he passed away after I graduated, I never reconciled with my mom. But Dani and Sean are my spiritual family. I trust them with just about everything."

Robert thought about it for a while. "I guess you're right. My family is a tight-knit unit; we went everywhere together. Even when Cheryl went off to college, she commuted, so there wasn't much of a disruption. Our unit wasn't broken up until I left for Georgia Tech. I guess a lot changed in the seven years I was gone."

Guilt hit Robert as he considered how early decisions might have impacted the current situation. His eyes began to well up again.

Sensing the gravity of his sadness, Kim assured Robert, "Babe, you didn't cause this. We didn't know what was going on. We'll get through it."

"I don't think you understand. This changes a lot! Things at work have been going so well. There have been talks about inviting me to be part of a leadership program. If I get in, this program will have me traveling all over the country. There will be opportunities for promotion; I mean, this opportunity is once-in-a-lifetime. I feel it will change our lives. But now, I don't know if I should do it."

"I hear you, babe. Let's put this into perspective, though. Looking back, you wouldn't have had this job and be in the position you are had you not torn your ACL at NBA camp. I know it was your dream to play in the league. It was at the tips of your fingers, and you weren't able to play one game. I always felt there was something more for you. Just look, you get two phenomenal breaks. God loves you, babe. It will be good to step away from the house for a little bit and talk it out in a safe space with trusted friends."

"I guess. I trust you, of course. Sean and Kim are great. Maybe if we get there before Joe and Linda, we can talk about it. I don't know if I'm ready to have everyone all in our business."

"Robert, you never know if someone else has gone through something similar. They might have ideas of things to consider and people to see. But I respect your feelings and will follow your lead."

"Thank you, love. I appreciate that. It's just so much to think about." Robert grabbed another tissue and wiped his eyes. "Okay, we're here ten minutes early. I don't see Joe's car. Let's go in and talk to Sean and Dani before they arrive."

Robert jumped out of the car and walked around to open the door for Kim. She hurried from the car. "I'm right behind you." Kim reached her arm to pull Robert closer as they walked to the front door. "I think we only have a couple of minutes. You know Joe and Linda like to be on time." Kim closed her eyes, looked up, and said a small prayer as Robert reached for the doorbell.

Chapter 3 - Joe & Linda's Ride to Small Group

Meanwhile, on the other side of town and headed to the same location, Linda saw they were getting closer to Sean and Dani's house. She contemplated reaching for the temperature controls to cool off.

Linda fidgeted with the belt on her outfit, ensuring the bow looked perfect. "How do you want to tell the group?" she asked.

"You know me, sweetie. I'm one to just rip off the band-aid, say it like it is, and rush in headfirst. You have a more nuanced, controlled approach. Whatever way you want to tell them, I'm okay with it. Honestly, while it affects our whole family, this is your news to share."

"Thank you, Joe. I do appreciate you saying that. I'll think of the right words to say and wait for the timing to be just right. Now…about Joey." Linda's tone dropped as she reached up and twisted the dial, lowering the temperature on her side.

"I think Joey senses something is about to change. We have to tell him this week." Joe's voice softened as they broached the sensitive subject. He glanced at Linda before continuing, "He's been talking about lacrosse camp this summer, and we need to figure out if they even play lacrosse in the Chicago suburbs."

Linda sighed. "Ugh, don't remind me about that; I think that's what pains me so much. Lacrosse is his first love, and I'm feeling really guilty about forcing his first big break-up."

"Linda, sweetie, don't take it that far. Yes, it's a big change, moving from Maryland to Illinois. Yes, it will impact the family. But I think it'll be for the good. We don't see it yet, we don't understand how it will work out, but I have this feeling about it."

"Joe, you're always so optimistic. I love that about you. But I don't think Joey will see it that way, and that's what I'm so worried about." She adjusted the vent, directing the air onto her neck, her voice filled with panic. "I'm afraid he's going to see it the wrong way and take out his feelings on me."

"What way do you think he'll see it?"

"He'll be mad at me and blame me for all the changes happening to our family and to him. This town, his friends. This is all that he knows, and we're uprooting him. I'm uprooting him."

Joe looked over and saw a red tint fill Linda's eyes.

"Yes, your opportunity is the reason we're moving. However, I think this is also an opportunity for a life lesson. As a man, he'll have to learn to work through major situations like this. On one hand, I'm glad we're here to help him through it. In a few years, he'll be off to college. He may not recognize it now, but he'll use the skills he learned in this moment to transition to whatever school he'll be going to." Joe seized upon that moment to insert some levity to break the tension. "Speaking of which, what's the latest college he's talking about? Is it still Duke, which is ranked number one in lacrosse?"

Relieved his plan worked, Linda's deep gaze broke as she formed a tiny smile and chuckled. "I think it's Maryland, College Park. He may end up coming back here for school!" Linda adjusted in the seat as she turned back towards Joe. "Over the years, I think I may have suppressed my feelings and created this self-imposed monument of never moving our family. I never really talked with my parents about how all the moves made me feel. Our generation didn't bring these things up, and we had to live with the consequences of those decisions. None of this was on my radar!"

Joe continued to lighten the mood. "Look, this talk has me thinking about empty nest life. He's over at Nasir's house for the night. We could call Sean and Dani and say one of us is sick."

"Joe..." Linda rolled her eyes. The high pitch of her tone suggested she understood the hint but remained centered on her anxious thoughts. "You're too much sometimes." She shifted her weight to lean in towards Joe and grabbed his arm. "I see what you're doing. You're trying to settle my mind like you always do by getting me to think about something else."

"What?" Joe said in a cagey tone.

"I moved about eight times from elementary school through high school. I hated it, and it was so hard to make friends. I made a promise to myself that I'd never let that happen to my kids. And now, I'm breaking that promise." Linda's vision blurred as tears welled.

"Sweetie, stop being so hard on yourself. Give yourself some grace. You've reached one of the top positions at your company here in Maryland. If you want to grow in your career, you have to relocate sites."

"Yes, that's true, Joe, and for so long, I suppressed that desire to move up. For the first ten years of my career, I watched as my leaders promoted people with less experience ahead of me, advancing them over me. I focused on my team, performing the best work I could provide. I was content with my job; I would be with them for 20 years. This was it, until Joey at least finished high school. Three years ago, my VP, Malcolm, first hinted to me to consider other opportunities, but I never pursued them."

Linda dabbed tears with a tissue from her purse, careful not to smudge her makeup. She straightened, her voice gaining confidence as she continued. "Then, when he left and Gabriella backfilled him, she saw the same performance. She was relentless and didn't back down as easily. She sensed I wanted to grow and decided to help make it happen for me."

"That's two vice presidents who both saw the high potential within you, encouraging you to move up. Incredible! It's what I saw the first moment I laid eyes on you."

"You know how to make me blush." Linda rubbed Joe's arm, signaling a drop in her anxiety. "Not one vice president, but two. And not being asked twice but three times. I couldn't help but notice it personally and challenge the promise I made to myself."

"Geez, this never happens," interrupted Joe. "We're going to be ten minutes late because of this. We always miss this train. What are the odds? The schedule must be off," Joe calmly added, hypnotized by the dozens of railcars passing by. "We're just a few blocks away from Sean and Dani's. Tell me the plan again. You know I'm a little dense. Are we bringing up the job change and worries about Joey, or just the job change?"

The arm rubbing stopped. Linda sat up straight in the seat to clear her mind. She took a deep breath and held it for a count of five. Then, she slowly exhaled through her nose for an additional count of five. "I feel we need to bring up both. Naturally, we're leaving our friends of over ten years in a little over a month. But the time we've shared has been such a blessing. We've helped each other through rough times over these years. I feel this is one of those moments where the wisdom of the group will define the right approach."

Joe and Linda sat in silence for the remainder of the drive. A few minutes later, the red flashing lights stopped pulsing, and the arm barriers blocking the tracks lifted. Linda looked out the window, practicing in her mind how she would reveal the news to her friends.

"Okay, sweetie, we're here. Oh, look. Robert and Kim are here already. This isn't like them. Usually, they're like twenty minutes late."

Chapter 4 - The Arrival

Concurrently, the fragrance of garlic permeated the air as Sean moved about his kitchen, putting the final touches on dinner. Dani put out the place settings, placing the forks and knives around the beautifully decorated dinner table.

"It's about time for Joe and Linda to arrive, and you know Robert and Kim are always late," said Dani. "So, maybe we should put the bread in the oven now?"

Sean paused for a moment, tilting his head in thought. "Usually, I'd agree with you. However, I have a strange feeling we'll need to delay a bit. This morning, during my quiet time in the Bible, I was led to read Acts 16. This is the chapter where Paul and Silas were planning to go to Asia to spread the word. With every attempt, the Lord prevented them from going. God had another plan in mind for them. I sense we'll need to be flexible with our plan for the evening, as well.

"Okay, honey, I hear you. However, we have to get through the planned material. We're on chapter four and have about five more chapters of the marriage book to get through."

"Noted, darling. I have the questions prepared that I want to ask." Sean smiled. "I'm curious how Joe will answer one question about 'walking in faith.' I'm so proud of how he's opened up over the years."

"Yes, me too. I love the growth and how it's impacted their marriage."

"Real quick, before everyone arrives, let's say a prayer," Sean suggested. "Father God, we thank you for who you are. We thank you for being in total control. We thank you for allowing us to steward these couples and pour into them, demonstrating the love of Christ. We are praying for travel mercies as they come from different directions. Lord, your word says that when two or more are gathered, you show up. Lord, we ask that you show up in a mighty way. Show up in a way that only you know how. Use Dani and me as your vessels to speak to and bless Joe, Linda, Robert, and Kim. Open our hearts and minds to what you have for us. I pray that at the end of the day, everyone leaves more aligned with you, seeking a deeper relationship with you, trusting more in you. It is in Jesus' name we pray, Amen."

Dani then walked into the living room to turn on the game for when the guests arrived. As she changed the channel, the doorbell rang.

"Right on time, I'll get it."

She reached for the deadbolt and opened the door. Beginning in her usual high octave greeting voice, "Hey Li-" and caught herself mid-word correcting herself, "Kim! Robert! How are you?!" Dani did her best to hide her mix-up. She masterfully concealed her perplexed state, thinking to herself, *Something is off*.

"Dani, so good to see you! We aren't too early, are we?" Kim said as she stepped into the warm foyer.

"Well, you're here sooner than normal, but that's great. Come in," Dani said with a smirk as she reached and hugged Kim. As Robert followed behind, she extended her arm to include him in the hug. "Honey, Robert and Kim are here!"

Dani's shorter frame caused her to overlook the dried stains of tears on Robert's cheek. "It smells so good in here. Did Sean cook?"

"Yes! He made his infamous lasagna."

"But I smell something else...something sweet."

"Nothing gets past you; that other smell you detect is a lemon pound cake recipe that I'm trying out," Dani explained. "My grandmother gave my mom the recipe. She's made it all these years and thought it was time to pass it on to me." She closed the door. "So, I'm letting you be my taste testers. I know my friends will give me honest feedback."

Robert's dry smile did well to mask his emotional turmoil. "How's Mel doing? Is he still working on his crossover? Where is he?"

"He's been working on it for the last month since you showed him how to do it." Dani then chuckled, "He's upstairs playing video games."

Robeert smirked as he said, "If he's going to do it, I want to show him how the best, Allen Iverson, did it."

Dani walked through the living room, around the plush couches, and into the kitchen to check on the rest of the food. Kim took a seat on the couch and glanced at the TV. After checking on her poundcake, Dani looked back into the living room and noticed that Robert had walked past the TV, ignoring the basketball game, and was now sitting at the dining room table.

Sean also noticed Robert's unusual body language and glanced at Kim. *They're usually so joyful and lighthearted at these monthly gatherings*, he thought. *Tonight, there seems to be a heavy burden weighing them down.* A few minutes later, Robert got up and walked to the bathroom.

"Kim! So good to see you!" Sean shouted warmly. "Is everything okay with Robert? I'd hug you, but as you see, I have my hands full."

The extended delay in Kim's reply said everything without her having to utter a word. Her lip tightened, and the way she glanced in Robert's direction said enough to confirm Sean's suspicions. "I'll wait for Robert to come out," she said. "But we're going through a situation, and we need your help."

The vague response didn't help either Sean or Dani. Dani's attention shifted to Kim to scan for clues regarding their dilemma. Her eyes darted to her hand for a ring check and then to her outfit and accessories. Nothing provided a clue to help her identify the issue.

"Kim, how did going through the homework assignment work for you and Robert? Did it spark meaningful discussion, and did you use the communication tools we learned about?" Dani probed to see if she would reveal any additional details.

"We had several amazing conversations about our financial future together. The recommended tools really helped us stay calm through our discussion, which can typically get heated."

Dani threw another signal to see if she could observe more body language. "Wonderful! I'm glad it's working for you. The next step is to develop a plan and maybe discuss family planning." Coming up empty, she felt comfortable touching on kids. "It must almost be time for your anniversary," said Dani. "You and Robert were married in the fall, right? Aren't you approaching three years?"

Kim's face lit up, and she smiled before she could get the words out. "Yes, this October will be three years." She turned her head in the direction of the bathroom and saw Robert returning.

Dani saw sadness replace the joy on Kim's face.

"Robert, what's going on, brother?!" Sean said to raise the spirits of the room. "How's work?"

Robert welcomed the momentary distraction from life's worries. "Work is great. I'm working on a big project that will help me build my business skills. I'm also being considered for a leadership program. But we're facing other changes." He thought he could mask his feelings, but saying those things out loud choked him up. He inadvertently let his guard down.

Distracted by the timer for the cake going off, Sean didn't catch the inflection in Robert's voice. But Dani grabbed it as a much-needed clue into what was going on.

"That's amazing, Robert! I'm happy for you. Tell me more about these changes!" Dani said.

A swirl of emotion filled Robert's head. Five seconds felt like five hours of unanswered questions. Where to start? What to say? Would he break down into an emotional blob? He was about to blurt the first thing that came to mind. "My da..."

However, Robert was interrupted by the doorbell.

Part II - The Rupture

Chapter 5 - Now That Everyone's Here

The interruption allowed Robert to pivot. "Sean! Did you just see that play?"

Dani opened the door with a warm, melodic soprano. "Hello, Linda and Joe! We're so excited you're here. We love getting together with our favorite couples. Come on in, Kim and Robert are already here. Sean is pulling the cake out of the oven for me."

"Dani, what did you make this time? You're not helping me fit into these clothes." Linda chuckled as she kissed Dani on the cheek.

"If it's anything like the other cakes or cookies you make, I can tell you before you give me a taste; it's out of this world!" Joe proclaimed as he walked into the living room and shook Robert's hand. His eyes were fixed on the television, which displayed the opening minutes of the playoff game.

"Joe, Linda, so good to see you! Happy anniversary! You've been married fifteen years, right?" Sean strolled from the kitchen and hugged Linda. He made his way over to Joe, where he was met with a warm embrace. "How's Joey?"

Joe's bright voice warm with pride responded, "Thank you. Yes, the 5th will make fifteen years. It goes by so quickly. Joey's great; he's getting ready for his sophomore year and has his eyes set on a varsity position on the lacrosse team." Joe's smile spread slowly, hoping his response was convincing enough to not provoke additional questions about Joey.

"That's so exciting! Linda, at what age did he start staying home by himself?" Dani inquired from the kitchen. "Sean seems to think Mel can stay home by himself at eleven, but I don't think I'm ready for him to grow up and be that mature just yet."

"I know what you mean. It was around eleven or twelve when we introduced that change. At fifteen, he's a professional." Linda tilted her head in thought.

"So, is Joey home now?" Dani inquired.

Joe quickly added, "Tonight, he's sleeping at a friend's house. This is a date night for us." Joe glanced provocatively at Linda and smiled.

"Easy, Tiger; we have a few things we need to talk about this evening. We could use some advice from all of you to help us process them."

"Sure, we'd be happy to help." Sean moved around the coffee table towards Kim, extending his arms to hug her. "I didn't properly greet you earlier." He then reached his hand towards Robert to shake it. This time, he noticed all the signs.

"Robert, something isn't right. What's going on? You two don't seem like yourselves this evening," Sean probed.

Robert fixed his face and forced a smile. He thought to himself, *How could I have wasted time in the bathroom trying to hype myself up?* Aloud, Robert said, "Oh, no, man. It's nothing. I was a little frustrated that we got out of the house late, and I missed the tip-off."

Joe walked in the direction of the TV and asked, "What's the score? I've been waiting for all these commercials to finish."

Robert met Joe halfway, shook his hand with a firm grip, and continued, "The score is 24-21. Both teams are playing great defense. You haven't missed much."

Kim embraced Linda, gave her the expected air kiss, and hugged Joe. Dani, seizing on the moment while everyone was standing, ushered the couples to the dining room table.

"Sean, dinner smells amazing! I'm going to miss your cooking," Joe blurted out in a moment of weakness. Linda's eyes expanded as wide as the dinner plates, and she quickly shot Joe a frantic look for talking so carelessly.

Sean's head tilted slightly, not letting the hastily shared words go unnoticed. He was already attuned to Kim and Robert's strange behavior. Now, Joe's comment had no chance of being overlooked.

Sensing Linda's discomfort, Dani quickly directed Sean. "Honey, would you please pray over the food?"

"Sure, please bow your heads," Sean started. "Heavenly Father, we thank you for this time of fellowship. We thank you for the friendship we have with these two amazing couples. We don't take for granted all the blessings of our marriages. We have been a spiritual family for one another through good times and bad, and we thank you. Lord, I ask that you bless each family represented here this evening. Bless the hands that prepared the food and bless the food itself for the nourishment of our bodies. This we ask in Jesus' name, Amen."

"Amen," responded everyone around the table.

Seizing an opportunity to deflect attention from his own issues, Robert quickly noted, "Am I the only one who heard the word 'miss'? What's going on, Joe? Linda?"

Clearly embarrassed with the clumsy reveal, Linda started to explain. "This wasn't how I wanted to share the news."

"Out with it already." Kim chimed in quickly, forgiving any missteps.

Joe smiled and looked at Linda. "Sweetie, I'm excited about it, but this is really your good news to share."

Chapter 6 - We're All Ears

The joy in Linda's voice filled the room, "Okay, okay. A few weeks ago, I was called into the office of the Vice President of Operations. At first, I was nervous that I'd done something wrong. She quickly brushed those thoughts aside. The VP explained how she was pleased with the performance of my team and the miraculous turnaround we achieved."

"I'm sure she was," Kim added, piling onto the excitement.

Linda revealed her confidence with the group as she continued. "She also asked my thoughts about the larger team and strategies we could implement to prepare for expanded growth in the upcoming years. I shared a few ideas I had, which impressed her further."

"And????" Dani was leaning in towards Linda, hanging onto every word.

"And it led to an interview for a promotion. I was selected to be the director of the project implementation team." Linda squealed out loud as she raised her hands in celebration.

The table erupted in joyous, celebratory clapping. "Oh, wow! Linda, we're so happy for you!" Sean said with a big smile.

Dani began serving the food. Kim reached for her water and took a sip. Before she could put the glass down, Robert grabbed his, mirroring his wife, gulping down some water. He scanned the table.

"That's not all of it," Linda continued. "This promotion will require us to relocate to the Midwest." Her smile flattened.

"What?!" Kim gasped.

Linda's throat began to close as she revealed, "We haven't shared the news with Joey yet. I know he's going to be devastated. His friends, his school, his church, lacrosse. Life in College Park is all he knows." The mixed emotions swelled up in Linda's eyes, and tears trickled as she contemplated the rippling effects of her decision.

Dani, forever optimistic, maintained her bright smile. "We'll miss you, but that's fantastic news!" She reached for Linda to comfort her. "It's a big move, and there will be many changes. However, it will be good for your family in ways that have yet to be revealed. Sean and I know about these major changes, don't we, honey?"

"Indeed, we do," Sean confirmed.

"Thank you for your kind and reassuring words." Linda tried to smile. However, her fear was in full control. The hesitancy in her voice made it clear that it was hard for her to accept. "I just don't know if Joey will see it the same way. What will we say? How can we help him process this? Joe and I are still cloudy about whether we made the right decision."

Lifting his fork casually, Robert added, "I'll be sad to see you leave. I love your family. Kim and I look up to all of you. There are life experiences you've gone through and counseled us through that have been invaluable in the past." Robert's feelings couldn't be contained. He thought to himself, *Maybe I should bring up my situation. What should I –*

"That's right!" Kim added as she nudged Robert out of a daze.

Robert placed his hands on the table and fondly declared, "The truth is, this isn't about the rest of us missing you. This is about the opportunity God has created for your family. I'm sure Joey will get over it eventually; he's young and doesn't understand everything. AND I love Chicago. So, you know Kim and I will come to visit!"

Sean replied, "Robert's correct. Joey will learn to understand and accept the decision. It will just take time. He'll realize that it's all part of God's plan. It reminds me of a period early in our marriage, when I was working as a marketing executive. I was fairly new to the team, thriving, meeting my deadlines, contributing to the success of the company." Sean's posture tightened as he proudly recalled the past. "Everything was phenomenal. I even recall having conversations with some of my peers about staying with the firm as a long-term prospect. I honestly saw my future there in the C-suite one day." He stopped talking and took a deep breath.

"It's okay, Sean," Dani reassured him.

His shoulders sank. In a dejected tone, Sean shared, "Then, out of the blue, I was called into my manager's office, where they explained the company wasn't doing as well as I thought. They needed to reduce expenses, which ultimately led to them letting me go." He added in a quiet, mournful tone, "Dani and I were trying to start a family. There was no way I thought that was possible now. My world was completely rocked!"

"Oh, Sean. I'm so sorry to hear about that," said Linda. "Why would they let you go? They were fools for making that decision!" she added with righteous indignation.

"Thanks, Linda." Sean smiled, "But the truth is, I had to leave. I didn't know it at the time. Yes, I was flourishing in my role, and yes, I was happy. Still, there was something better, something more special for me that I wasn't aware of at the time. And frankly, I don't know if I would have willingly given up my job to acquire what I have now." Sean fiddled with his hands as his elbows rested on the table's edge. "I wasn't mature enough to recognize it then. Dani had to be the sole provider during the eight months I was unemployed."

"Wow, man," said Joe, pointing his fork and knife at his plate, "I never would've known. I thought you were always in the catering business."

Reflecting on the moment caused a small lump to catch in Sean's throat. "I didn't see it then, but looking back now, I clearly see God was looking out for us. During that time, I think I hit rock bottom." All eyes were fixated on Sean's every word. As he shared, his jaw began to tighten, "I'd been one of the top recruits coming out of college, and now, I couldn't find a job? During that time, I think God and I had it out! I was mad at him. How could he let that happen to me?"

Robert's body straightened, leaned in closer, and subtly mirrored Sean. "How did you handle it?"

Sean continued, "My whole life, I was the good kid; I did everything I was supposed to. I followed the rules, studied, wasn't out late, respected my parents, and respected my girlfriend, who eventually became my wife. I saw what some of my friends and peers in the workplace were doing then, and I didn't agree with it. Morally, I couldn't align with those things, and yet, I was the one who was let go. To me, that wasn't fair, and God needed to give me answers so it could make sense to me." The emotions from the experience returned to Sean as he visualized his low moment.

Dani added, "At his lowest, it seemed that Sean was in a full-blown depression, and I was worried, so I reached out to his mother for help. The only thing that can rival the love of a healthy marriage is the love a mother has for her son. Linda, you know what I mean." Linda made eye contact and gestured in the affirmative.

Sean composed himself and continued, "That's true. After Dani reached out to her, my mom shared a story about the Mighty Mountain with me. It was odd; I'd never heard the story before. She explained that her mother, Gigi, shared this story with her before I was born. And Gigi heard it from her father when she was an adolescent. Maybe she was waiting for just the right time, and that was it."

Joe stared at Sean, puzzled. Robert's body language shifted, and he lowered the bite he was about to take when Sean said the word 'father.'

Sean continued. "*'The Mighty Mountain'* was the story of a mountain that discovered its purpose over time. It was meant to show me I was part of a larger plan. I was shaken out of my lowest point after Mom told me the story. By no means was my condition immediately changed. Still, it gave me a perspective that I didn't have before, and it inspired me to return to God with a revised posture."

"Do you think this Mighty Mountain story would help Joey?" Joe's eyebrow raised, and he lifted his arms with his palms close together, questioning. "I just don't know where to start. I don't know what to say. I'm excited about Linda getting this opportunity. It's been a long time coming."

"Aww, thank you, Hun." Linda melted as she placed her hand on his arm.

Joe continued, "It's hard for me to empathize with him, as I had to relocate several times during my adolescence. I had to quickly build rapport at each new school I moved to. Maybe that's why I got into consulting."

"It sounds like the story might help," Kim added, but she was thinking more of Robert. Kim quickly took a bite of the lasagna so as not to look desperate.

"Definitely, it can," Sean responded confidently. "It wasn't until three months after I heard the story that it started making sense. I honestly thought the lull was a phase. I was optimistic that my dry spell was about to turn the corner, and it didn't. Nine months in is when I gave up all hope." Sean paused again but remained confident.

Robert hesitantly said, "No, Sean. Not you. That's hard to believe."

"Yes, I'd given up. After hearing the story, I began to see things more clearly. Admittedly, I had a bit of a pride issue. You heard me describe my character when I was younger. That pride clouded my judgment and perspective on other priorities. If I'd remained in that job, I wouldn't be the man sitting before you today. I'd probably be off working on some marketing campaign, putting in crazy hours because that's what I saw the others doing."

Perplexed and in disbelief, Joe said out loud what everyone was thinking. "That doesn't even sound like you."

Linda and Kim glanced at one another, wondering where Sean's explanation was going. "I was out of work for almost 18 months. The last two months of my depression, things were getting better. I discovered things about myself, such as my passion for cooking and serving. During the last two months, I found healing through the meals I made for my wife."

"My wardrobe didn't appreciate him like I did," Dani joked.

"My catering business, the success and joy I've experienced over the last 15 years, wouldn't have existed had it not been for this unforeseen circumstance. This, us, around the table, our friendship, would not have existed. This is all part of God's plan for me. I feel like I'm operating in my gift and so much better for it," Sean proclaimed.

Chapter 7 - Can't Hold It in Anymore

Sean's poised assertion was enough to shake Robert's emotional façade loose. He looked down and used two fingers from each hand to massage the stress from his temples.

Dani noticed, took a bite, and casually asked, "Robert, what's going on with you? There's been something off with you and Kim since you arrived. C'mon, tell us. This is a safe space. What's up?"

Robert put down his fork and released a long, exhaling breath. "Today, my sister called, telling me to come over to my parents' house. When we got there, my da – ." He couldn't finish his sentence before an emotional flood of questions and what-if scenarios overwhelmed his mind. Kim dropped her utensils onto the plate and put her arm around Robert to rub his back. The others, unsure of the required response, were on the edges of their seats in anticipation.

Kim carefully added the needed details, "Unbeknownst to us, Robert's dad has been showing early signs of dementia for the past few months. Today was a pivotal moment for the family. He wandered from the house and left his phone on top of his car. His keys were on the stairs, and the front door was wide open. We spent three hours looking for him and finally found him about a mile and a half away, walking down Renaissance Way. He was genuinely lost and confused. He's lived in that house and neighborhood longer than Robert's been alive. I can't understand how those memories are gone."

"Oh, I'm so sorry to hear that, Robert!" said Dani. "I can't pretend to know the weight of what you're carrying."

Tears trickled down Kim's face. She grabbed a napkin and dabbed the corners of her eyes, continuing. "We were so scared that something happened to him. We feared the worst. Once we found him, we brought him home. We came here just to have a safe place to think about what happened. Later, we'll return to talk about a family plan."

In between sniffles, Robert revealed, "I feel so guilty and selfish. I was about to change jobs for a better opportunity that requires more travel and time away from family. In light of this situation, I don't know if that's the best decision right now."

"You shouldn't feel guilty or selfish," suggested Joe. "You didn't know it was happening, and if you saw some signs, certainly didn't think it would progress so quickly."

"Well, I can't tell you what the right decision is," declared Sean. "That's something you, Kim, and the rest of your family will have to pray about. I'm confident God will reveal in his own unique way the right course of action for you, just like he did for me."

"Oh my," added Linda. "I thought our situation was difficult, but I can only imagine what's going through your minds right now. You know Joe and I'll be praying for you. Please know we'll do whatever we can for you while we're here."

"Thanks, Linda. That really means a lot to us," replied Kim.

Looking to add some humor to the heavy moment, Robert quipped, "In all this sharing, my food got cold. I can't let Sean's God-given talents go to waste. I'm putting this delicious lasagna in the microwave. Can I heat up anyone else's?"

Joe smirked and added before taking his next bite, "You know, just when Sean was about to tell us the story, all these revelations sidetracked him from sharing it. Does anyone else have something to share before Sean tells us the story? Speak now or forever hold your peace!"

No one in the room could contain their laughter. It was much needed to get past the last few minutes. Once everyone was composed and Robert returned from reheating his food, Sean started.

"This is how my mom explained the story to me."

In that instant, Sean remembered the sinking desperation he felt after months of rejection. The smell of wanton apathy drew him back to the low place where he vowed he'd never return. This time, he knew exactly where to find the path out of the pit. His time in the pit prepared him to be a helpful guide. He could instruct his friends on where to step and which traps to avoid, leading them towards freedom.

"She told me it was important to share all the details," he said, "so listen carefully."

Chapter 8 - The Mighty Mountain

When the Earth was created, a tall mountain was formed. It was perfectly situated in a location surrounded by other mountains, but they weren't quite as tall or wide. When this particular mountain looked down, it saw a blanket of trees followed by a vibrant ocean of beautifully colored flowers. When it looked up, it saw an endless royal blue sky, which almost matched the shade of blue that composed the body of water in the distance.

For the first few days, the mountain observed the bright yellow sun ascend on its left side and descend on its right. The mountain heard the wind whistle as it rushed past and occasionally felt the rain spray against its face. This unique mountain wondered to itself, *Why am I here? What should I be doing?*

An unusually calm breeze wafted by with a gentle whisper and said, "Wait and be obedient."

The mountain questioned back, "How long? Obedient to what? Who am I following?"

However, the breeze with a gentle voice disappeared.

Over time, the mountain observed that it possessed unique abilities that the other mountains didn't have. It could stretch high and wide, twist and contort itself. When the mountain looked low, it saw the trees and flowers. It thought to itself that they were so beautiful. At the edge of its vision, it noticed that a few of the flowers were drying out from the sun. While it stared in awe, a strong breeze passed, pulling the dry, withered flowers from the ground, and blowing them away. At that moment, the mountain realized how vulnerable the flowers and trees were and decided they needed protection. The mountain declared, "I will protect them from the ominous elements." That tall, mighty mountain stood proudly above the valley.

The sun rose every day, lighting up the green grass that blanketed the mountain's base, complementing the bronze-colored rock. Some days, the sun shone so brightly that the grass and flowers below in the valley started to dry out and burn. On those days, the mighty mountain stretched its peak so high that it cooled the grass and the flowers with the shadow it cast on the valley below.

On other days, the wind gently blew breezes that made the leaves in the trees, flowers, and grasses wave back and forth in the valley below. Some days, the wind blew so strongly that it threatened to push down the trees and pull up the flowers in the valley. On those days, the mighty mountain stretched wide, making the wind blow more slowly through the trees, flowers, and grasses in the valley below.

On other days, rain lovingly fell, watering the trees, flowers, and grasses in the valley below. Some days, so much rain fell that it tried to wash away the trees, the flowers, and the grasses in the valley. On those days, the mighty mountain shifted and thinned the rushing rivers of water into trickling streams around the trees, flowers, and grasses.

Proudly, the mighty mountain stood for many years. It was happy with protecting the valley below. That was its job.

Then, on an unusual day, something unexpected happened to the mighty mountain. It wasn't burned by the sun, blown away by the wind, or washed away by the rain. An earthquake struck and injured the mountain!

This earthquake shook the ground and created a small crack. That crack eventually developed into a large one, causing the peak to break off the mighty mountain. As it rolled down the hill, it tumbled and toppled into smaller rocks that broke it further. Boom – rumble – crack – bam!

Just before it reached the valley's lowest point, the once-mighty mountain hit a final rock that shattered this once-magnificent peak into five jagged pieces. They now resided in the valley below.

The five broken pieces lay helpless, beat-up, and sad in the valley. Day after day, year after year, those elements that the mountain had overpowered exacted their revenge on the mountaintop. The sun beamed down directly, drying the pieces and making them withered and brittle.

The unwavering wind blew the pieces together, causing them to chip away at each other. The unshielded rain formed into quickly moving streams that collected smaller stones and sand, further wearing down the pieces. This cycle continued for many years until only five smooth stones remained.

The five smooth stones looked at each other and shared many thoughts. *What good are we now? We used to create long, stretching shadows, break up gusts of wind, and stand firm as shields from the driving rain. Now, we are part of the valley, at the lowest point of existence, washed down to nothing but smooth rocks.*

Then, one day, after a heavy rain drenched the land, a young man passed through and interrupted the silent valley. As he walked, he reaffirmed himself. He stated, "The Lord is my shepherd! I will fear no evil! The Lord IS my shepherd!"

That voice came from a young man named David. He picked up the five smooth stones from the stream and put them into his bag. Then, armed only with his shepherd's staff, sling, and stones, he started across the valley to fight a giant.

Holding his sling, David grabbed one of the stones. He hurled it with the sling and defeated the giant. David had saved his people! At that moment, the once mighty mountain found great joy.

"He picked up five smooth stones from a stream and put them into his shepherd's bag. Then, armed only with his shepherd's staff and sling, he started across the valley to fight the Philistine."

1 Samuel 17:40

Part III - The Refinement & Redemption

Chapter 9 - Who Is in the Center?

Joe and Linda held hands. Kim's head leaned on Robert's shoulder as her left hand grabbed his arm. Everyone's eyes were wide open around the table, and their minds were racing with random thoughts.

"Sean, I never saw that coming. That's such a powerful story. Maybe I'm dense, but I didn't see the connection until the last line," Joe added, attempting to make a joke that fell flat.

"Yes, Joe. We always tell the story from David's perspective," said Sean. "We speak and analyze his courage about facing giants and the victory that comes from it. We know that David eventually becomes the king after God's own heart. So, it's easy to see the destiny that comes from walking in purpose. It's not until you consider the story from another vantage point that you glean something even more powerful from it."

Dani added, "I'd never thought about the stones and what it took to get them there. They were in place when David went searching for the right stones needed at that moment."

Kim struggled to see how the story could help her and Robert. "Sean, you said this story could help Joey. I'm having a hard time seeing how this could apply."

"Sure, that's a fair question, Kim," Sean started. "I've had sixteen years to really chew on the story and its application. I think, on the surface, the story centers around a mountain that feels its purpose is to protect some trees and flowers, but it was destined for something greater. It was borderline prideful, out of ignorance, more than anything else."

Joe assessed, "I can see how the story connected with you. The different applications come from how you understand the story and which of the characters you identify with and for what reason."

"What conclusions have you drawn in your time studying the story?" asked Linda.

"Well, for characters, you have the mountain, the sun, the wind, and the rain clouds, as well as the trees and grasses," said Sean. "Lastly, you have David. As I mentioned, we know the story from David's perspective. For my situation, when my mom shared the story with me, I mostly aligned with the Mighty Mountain. I'd been on top of my game and felt invincible. I was successful, with a clear, bright future ahead of me. At that moment in time, I felt like I was doing what I was made to do."

Joe brought his hand to his chin and rubbed it across his face, nodding his head. "Okay."

"Life couldn't get any better," Sean continued. "Beautiful wife, big house, money, success. The only thing I didn't have was kids, and I believed they would come just as easily. So, you can naturally see how, when I was let go, that was no different than the earthquake that devastated the mountain!"

"I think I follow," Linda responded. "So, because the change is happening to me, I should view myself as the Mighty Mountain? If I'm the mountain, then who is Joey? Is he the flowers that I'm protecting? Is Joe the wind? Help me understand."

"Linda, I think for simplicity's sake, I would center Joey as the Mighty Mountain." Sean leaned into the table with unhurried patience. "From his fifteen-year-old perspective, he's on top of the world, living his best life, doing the things he loves. The news about moving could be equivalent to the earthquake."

"Now I understand where I think you're going," said Joe. "But who am I, Sean? I feel like I could be the sun. I brighten up the spaces I'm in." Joe smiled lightheartedly. Scanning the room, Joe saw the others nod their heads in agreement, trying to anticipate where this was going.

Sean chuckled. "Yes, Joe, I feel your role is like the sun, wind, or rain." Sean added thoughtfully, "Those represent life and the constant forces of change. In the story, they have a clear and distinct purpose. Despite the mountain's best efforts, they actually did what they were supposed to do, which day after day was shaping the broken peak into the five smooth stones."

"I like that role; I can embrace that role!" Joe smiled.

Sean's gaze expanded to include Linda as he explained, "In the same way, you and Linda as his parents have the responsibility to love and guide him. You'll be there when other major events happen, day after day, further shaping his life, preparing him for his great moments."

"So, what could we tell Joey? I want to soften the blow as much as possible," Linda said in a gentle voice. By this time, Linda had resolved not to eat and merely focus on the lesson.

"Linda, the truth is, we don't know how Joey will respond," Dani admitted. "I didn't predict Sean hitting the lows that he experienced. But talking about it out loud, you and Joe should be in a better position to look for signs."

Kim added, "I think what you want Joey to internalize is that he's not alone. His mom and dad are there with him, God's with him, and He has a plan. It isn't always immediately clear, but put faith and hope in the fact that there is one."

Hearing the Mighty Mountain story, Robert couldn't get his family's current challenge out of his head. Images of the door left wide open flashed across his mind. A pain radiated across his shoulders as the muscles in his back tightened. It was the same tense feeling he had as he and Kim drove all over town scanning the neighborhood for his dad. Questions echoed in his head as bits and pieces of Sean's explanation snuck into his consciousness. *Am I in the center? Am I the mountain? Why is this happening to me?*

"It makes sense to me, Joe. At times, you can be a little windy," Robert chimed in as he took another forkful of lasagna.

The comforting nature of the conversation allowed Robert to temporarily escape the painful realities of the moment and joke with his friends. It was moments like these that made his mom's recommendation to go out and see them worthwhile.

"Sean, earlier you said, 'preparing him for his great moments.' What do you mean?" asked Linda.

"Good question. Linda, the truth is, we don't know what God's detailed plan is for us. We have faith he has one for us. Our faith is built on the idea of his word and our belief in God's character being the same yesterday, today, and tomorrow. For example, Jeremiah's statement to the exiles in Babylon, documented in the 29th chapter of Jeremiah, verse 11, is paraphrased as 'I know the plans I have for you. They are plans for good and not for disaster, to give you a future and a hope.' Does this make sense?"

"Kind of," Linda said with a bit of hesitation. "Please make it plain for me."

Patiently, Sean explained, "What I mean is, these plans could lead to a singular moment or towards several significant, impactful moments. I can't say with any level of confidence or accuracy what it would look like. When we look at the lives of the twelve disciples, they were invited to follow Jesus. He didn't tell them everything that would happen over the next three years or throughout the remainder of their lives. It would have influenced their decisions at the time. We must trust God, day by day."

"Prayerfully, my baby Joey is going to be part of many significant moments," Linda confidently replied.

Chapter 10 - What's Big For Some Is Small For Others

While Sean was expanding on the topic, Dani gazed at her husband in admiration. She added, "This revelation didn't come overnight. It wasn't a Moses mountaintop moment that was handed to us. It took years to come to this conclusion, and ultimately, the gift from God to finally see what was in front of us the whole time. I've learned the size of moments is relative. What's big for some is small for someone else. That's the beauty in it."

"Can you elaborate on that, Dani?" Kim asked.

"The first year, Sean was depressed. It took six months before I could convince him to get out of bed. Over that time, my career grew, and promotions sustained us. God had our backs the entire time. One of my coworkers invited us to their church. It had been almost a year when, strangely enough, Sean agreed to get up and go to church. It was a sermon about 'God working on your spirit.' Pastor Terrance used James chapter 1 as the basis of his message."

"You're right, darling. My mom had just shared the story with me before Christmas, and it was bouncing around in my head for three months. Something within urged me to get up and go. I'll never forget the first verse of James chapter 1. 'God blesses those who patiently endure testing and temptation. Afterward, they will receive the crown of life that God has promised to those who love him.' It was something about the testing and temptation in combination with the rocks being worked on by the elements."

"I think your test was pretty clear, but what about the temptation? How were you tempted?" Robert asked. Sean's story had grabbed his attention. Robert was desperately trying to align his situation with the story.

"First, Robert, my identity was tangled up in being this marketing executive," answered Sean. "Yes, it was a gift from God. Yes, I was great at it. However, there was a gap of sorts, something missing. I felt it but couldn't articulate it as clearly as I can now." Sean's eyes locked in on Robert's to make sure he was being understood. "So, when I lost my job, I was mourning the role, mourning the attention, and everything that came with it. The temptation arose from a desperate attempt to reclaim and recreate what was lost. Applying to hundreds of jobs, which I knew I was perfectly qualified for. I was obsessed with regaining the role to a fault. I was focused on the role and not God who gave me the role."

The information tossed into Robert's lap felt heavy. Not quite a burden, but questions began to rapidly formulate in his mind.

"What I didn't share is what changed within me," continued Sean. "You see, there was still more refinement required within my spirit. Like the stones, I had to endure more of the sun, wind, and rain. But it wasn't what you might expect. I joined a men's group at church. I was around many successful men, but their priorities were different than mine had been."

"How so?" Linda asked.

"They weren't successful men whose identities were defined by their accolades and material possessions. They were Christ-following men who, through their faith, were blessed with resources that would make a lasting impact in their family, the community where they lived, and in the world around them," Sean revealed. "This was the lesson I had to learn, and it was through spending time with them that I saw it modeled."

"Hmmmm," Robert muttered.

"I invited the group over one weekend, and a few of them were so impressed with my cooking that they basically forced me to cater different events they hosted. Fast forward, fifteen years later, I'm here," Sean concluded.

"There are many other details he excluded for brevity's sake, but had it not been for Sean's willingness to step out in faith, I don't know where we'd be right now," added Dani.

"What do you think, Linda?" Joe asked.

"To summarize," Linda began, "when a major change comes, and it challenges your identity, the first step is to ensure your identity is aligned with God, and you have a relationship with him. The second step is to explore the direction in which God is leading you, and the third step is to embrace the direction and walk in it purposefully."

"Exactly!" Sean affirmed.

Linda locked her right arm around Joe's and made deliberate eye contact with him. "So, Joey, Joe, and I have some work to do involving our son's relationship with God. I feel many of our conversations have been superficial. However, he's older now, and there's an opportunity to talk on a much deeper level." She nodded her head at Joe as she spoke, looking for confirmation. "The direction God has for him may not be easily identifiable now, but we can help him through the process."

"Sure, that's a great way to look at it," Sean agreed, nodding.

"Once he figures it out, he can lean in and take it one day at a time," concluded Linda.

Robert sat back in his chair. "And that's it?" he snapped in a lukewarm tone.

"Yes, Robert, more or less," Sean confirmed.

Kim began to smile, believing she'd heard the beginning of a plan leading towards a path of resolution for her husband.

What she couldn't see were the vivid thoughts flashing through Robert's mind. He saw visions of turning down future opportunities that had yet to be offered. The anticipated sadness and disappointment flooding his emotions were quickly flushed out to make way for the anger and resentment that were silently ready to be released.

Chapter 11 - We Can Be the Stones

The sense of ease Kim felt was interrupted by the tone of Robert's next statement. "I don't know, Sean. I'm –" He let out an exasperated sigh. "When I try to center myself, in my situation, I'm at a loss. I had what you described as my 'earthquake moment' years ago. I was supposed to be in the league. You were all supposed to be watching me on TV. But I'm here. I've accepted that wasn't God's plan for me. It took some time, but I got there. I was at peace with that plan ending, and I was on a different path."

Listening to Robert's voice decrescendo and begin to crack caused tears to well in Kim's eyes. "Oh, babe!"

Emotionally exhausted, Robert cried out, "I thought I was on God's plan, and things were going well. I told you all that I was getting opportunities to grow; my career is taking off. Everything was moving up. And then, this afternoon, I got a call that my father has moderately severe Alzheimer's disease."

Robert pinched the bridge of his nose, trying to relieve a feeling that wasn't easily shaken off. "He walked out of my childhood home, left the door open, and my family and I couldn't locate him for hours." Tears welled in Robert's eyes and began streaming down. Bitterly, he let out, "I don't know how to manage THIS earthquake."

Silence filled the dining room. Sean got up from the table. "I'm so sorry, Robert, I can't possibly fathom what you're going through." Sean's words to Robert were as empathetic as the hand he put on his shoulder.

Linda glanced at Joe, who was in just as much shock as she. Then, she shifted her eyes to Kim to see if she needed comfort. Linda's eyes continued over to Dani to take any cues from her.

In his unease, Joe used the side of his fork to cut another small piece of lasagna, making a screeching sound. Linda nudged him to stop. "Huh?"

Dani seized the moment to share. "Robert, again, I'm sorry to hear about your father. I know that hearing such news and seeing its continued effects will often feel overwhelming. And I know you're processing a lot. If I may offer another perspective. Maybe you're not intended to be the mountain in this situation. Maybe you're the stone?"

Robert lifted his face from his hands. Kim stopped rubbing his back to dip a napkin in the water and gently wiped his face.

"What do you mean, Dani?" Kim inquired.

"I mean, as Robert shared, he's gone through an earthquake moment and is changing. However, what if he's just feeling the shaking, and the situation isn't intended to disrupt his course, but rather for him to be of use and assistance in the moment."

Sean sat up straighter, intrigued, and positioned his attention towards his wife. "Please say more."

"Well, when I was in college, I was on an engineering scholarship. I believed I would follow in my father's footsteps. However, the truth was that I struggled with higher-level math, and there wasn't any type of engineering that I loved. Long story short, I didn't do so well academically, lost my scholarship, and had to change majors."

Joe chipped away at the tension more with his playful tone. "How did that go over with your parents? How did your dad feel? I know he must have been sad."

"Joe, really???" retorted Linda, scolding him for taking it too far.

"I was devastated. I felt like I'd disappointed my dad and let my family down. For me, it was an earthquake moment. I was an 'A' student and was in an unfamiliar position. Fast forward several years, and I found a new career path. I met Sean while in law school, and things were solid."

Sean gave Dani an inquisitive look. He anticipated where she was going next with her story. He was surprised that he'd never considered it himself in his years of reflection over his career transition. Sean was awestruck when Dani finally concluded, "Just when I was up for junior partner at my law firm, Sean was let go. The increase in my salary didn't fully make up for Sean's contribution, but we weren't uncomfortable. I was the stone in that moment. It was many years of hard work, long days, and late nights. But I was there to help our family when they needed it. I was the stone that was used to defeat the giant that was attacking our marriage. Maybe that's your situation as well."

Linda examined everyone's disposition around the table, starting with Joe, to make sure he didn't do anything else to embarrass her. She sensed the tension was waning. Everyone's shoulders were relaxing. Robert was sitting up straighter. The stress must have been dissipating.

Kim's optimism began to regenerate as she shifted back in her seat, holding Robert's arm. "What do you think, babe? I feel like Dani made a great point."

Robert grabbed his cup, took a big gulp, and set the cup back down. "Thank you, Dani. Really. Thank you! Your words talked me down. I truly felt like I was spinning. Yes, Kim, I can embrace that perspective. The hardest part, in my mind, is that I'm not there yet. It's just beyond my fingertips."

Linda chimed in, "Robert, thinking about the story as Dani explained it, you and Kim could each be stones for this situation, working together to help your parents. I see your mom more like David. From the stories you've shared in the past, I know she's strong. But she may be looking for a unique type of help…help that only you can provide."

Joe added, "In an odd, providential way, maybe they're being prepared to be a stone for you and Kim." His half-joke became more serious, and he expanded on his thought. "Kim, you shared a few months back that you were worried and didn't have strong, stable, long-term relationships on your side of the family as models, since many family members have divorced. You're observing in real time what living out those vows 'In sickness and in health' means. I've heard it said that God can use tragedy and turn it into triumph."

Sean seized upon the moment to tie in a verse from the previous gathering's lesson. "Everyone, if you remember from last month, the verse centered around 1 Peter 4:10, 'Each of you should use whatever gift you have received to serve others, as faithful stewards of God's grace in its various forms.' As we look back on our lives and what we've experienced so far, these moments are shaping us for usefulness to one another. I know 'The Mighty Mountain' ended with a great victory over a menacing giant. However, there should be excitement about victory over any situation, great or small. And I firmly believe that is part of God's plan."

The conversation between the six friends continued for several more hours, building on points the others had made. Glancing at his watch, Robert commented, "My spiritual family, I want to thank each and every one of you for your wisdom and insights. I don't know what I would do without you. When I get back to my mom's house, I'm going to share the amazing story of the Mighty Mountain with my family. They have to hear this. Thank you for sharing it with us, Sean."

"Yes! Thank you, Sean and Dani, for opening up your home and your hearts," said Kim. "Dinner was amazing, and the dialogue was inspiring to me. I know that I never leave the same whenever I'm around you."

"Before you two leave, let me pray for all of us." Sean took Dani's hand and extended his hand towards the rest of their guests. Sean lowered his head and said, "Heavenly Father, we thank you this evening for being in the middle of our conversation. We thank you for the perfect plan that you have for each of us and the patience you have as you watch it fall into place, day by day. We stand in awe over how you've laid everything out. We don't understand everything as it happens or why it happens or why it happens to that person, but we trust you. We stand on your word that says all things that happen are for the good of those who believe. We trust that you have our best interests in mind at all times. Lord, we lift up Robert's father, who has been diagnosed with Alzheimer's disease. If it is your will, we are praying for miraculous healing, Lord, that only you can provide. We are praying for the doctors and specialists he and his family will be seeing over these next few months. We lift up his wife, pour into this woman who is taking care of her spouse. It's not easy. Bless the love and resources that go into the care she will provide. Lord, we lift up Robert and pray that he is being shaped into the stone that will provide victories for his family. Give him the strength to be a resource for his family.

"Lord, we lift up Joe and Linda. Give them the wisdom and words to speak to their son, Joey. We pray that you open his heart and ears to what they have to say. We know the transition will be tough, but we ask you to make it just a little easier for him. Lord, we pray for them as they move from Maryland to Chicago that the transition may be easy and without challenge.

"Bless each of the households represented here, Lord; we pray safe travel mercies as everyone returns home, that they find their houses are in order. All these things we pray in Jesus' name, Amen and amen."

Everyone raised their heads and began to exchange departing hugs. Without missing a beat, Joe took the opportunity to announce, "Kim and I have to head out as well. As I mentioned, we have a follow-on date, since the boy is sleeping over at his friend's house this evening."

"Ohhh, Joe," Linda started, "what am I going to do with you?" she laughed. The rest of the group joined in.

Afterward

I sincerely hope this book has spoken to you. My prayer in writing it was to create something that not only complements the children's version but also equips parents, grandparents, aunts, uncles, and mentors with language and perspective when the children in their lives face seasons of change.

While Sean didn't describe it this way in the story, a natural four-step pattern emerges that can help us make sense of change: **recognition, rupture, refinement**, and **revelation**. When you revisit the story, notice which step each character is walking through. As you reflect on your own life, use these words as anchors to help frame your journey.

The story is more than a parable; it's a mirror. Each character carries a piece of us, reflecting struggles, hopes, and the quiet courage it takes to move forward.

- For those like Kim, who we learn had a rupture moment in the past, as alluded to by the fact that she didn't have examples to draw from for marriage, you can still be a useful stone. While we didn't fully explore her refinement process, it is revealed that she possesses a gift of empathy that was given to her supernaturally. God's plan is not meant to overwhelm you but to help you grow, step by step.

- For those like Robert, whose dreams were once within reach only to be ruptured by loss or unexpected turns, don't let disappointment silence your hope. Even in grief and uncertainty, God surrounds you with people who carry what you cannot. He hasn't left you, and He will provide support in ways you may not yet see.

- For those like Linda, who recognize her strengths and quietly carry the weight of others and bury their own desires in the name of stability, let this be your reminder that protecting your family sometimes looks like stepping boldly into the opportunities God places before you. God is more than capable enough to handle blessings meant for you and your loved ones simultaneously.

- For those like Joe, who over time maintains his revelation that his gift is sensing tension, lifting burdens, and steering others back towards peace, never underestimate the ministry of presence. Humor, optimism, and steady words in anxious rooms are not small things; they are lifelines.

- And finally, for couples like Sean and Dani, who open their homes, share their table, and invest in others, your story shows us that the church is not confined to buildings, but is sustained through open doors, honest conversations, and meals shared in faith. Community survives and thrives when ordinary people make space for others.

Each of these lives, woven together, reminds us that the ground may shift, careers can end, loved ones may falter, moves and diagnoses may come, but God is faithful. And like the parable of "The Mighty Mountain," even in breaking, there is shaping. Even in loss, there is preparation for victory.

Just as David picked up five smooth stones, God equips us for victory against the giants we face in family, faith, finances, fitness, and friendships. These are the key areas of our lives where challenges arise, but also where God's provision and purpose can shine through.

Here is my charge to you: find your place in the story. Are you Linda, Robert, Kim, Joe, Sean, or Dani in this season? What lesson is God whispering to you through their journey?

And don't walk it alone. Bring someone with you. Share the parable. Talk about the questions it stirs. Let it guide your own conversations with your children, family, or small group.

I would be honored to walk this journey with you and hear how these stories speak into your life, your family, and your faith. Together, may we become people who don't just endure life's earthquakes, but who allow God to shape us into stones that defeat giants.

Remember this: the ground may shift, and the mountain may disappear, but what remains are sacred stones ready to be used for God's glory.

Acknowledgements

First and foremost, I thank God for giving me such an impactful story. Without His inspiration, there would be no *Mighty Mountain*.

To my wife and best friend, my girls, and friends – thank you for your love, patience, and encouragement. Your support kept me grounded and motivated. To those who first heard the parable and nudged me to create an adult version, your words were seeds that grew into this book.

I am grateful to my editor and beta readers, who sharpened the story and helped it resonate with a broader audience. Your wisdom, feedback, and honesty have been invaluable.

To my small groups over the years, thank you for being a community of faith, accountability, and encouragement. You reminded me that stories don't just live on pages; they live in people.

This book is also a reflection of everyone I've ever been in contact with in life. Like the sun, wind, and rain, each interaction has shaped and refined me into the stone I needed to be in order to write this book.

I dedicate the impact of this work to my father, who was a Mighty Mountain in my life. He raised me to be a good man, a faithful husband, and a loving father. Though he was not alive to see how I've carried those lessons forward, I believe he is watching from heaven, smiling at the return on the investments he made in me.

Finally, a special thanks to **Blkpawn Publishing** for helping to shape the vision of this story and allowing me to share it the way God first gave it to me.

Continue the Journey

Thank you for spending time with *The Mighty Mountain: When the Ground Beneath You Shifts*. My hope is that this story has spoken into your own journey of faith, change, and courage. But the journey doesn't have to end here.

- ❖ **Free Resources for You**
  We've created bonus materials to help you apply the lessons of *The Mighty Mountain* in your daily life:
  - **"Sacred Stones" Reflection Guide** — a short PDF with journaling prompts for personal or group study.
  - **7-Day Encouragement Email Series** — bite-sized devotions delivered straight to your inbox.
  - **Printable Verse Cards** — scriptures tied to the themes of courage, faith, and change you can keep on your desk, mirror, or Bible.
  - **Children's Activity Sheet** — a fun way for kids to engage with the parable alongside the adult story.
    Download for free at
    https://www.blkpawnpublishing.com/pages/mighty-mountain-content.

- ❖ **Visit Blkpawn Publishing**
  Explore more resources, devotionals, and stories that inspire at www.blkpawnpublishing.com.

- ❖ **The Children's Edition**
  Share the parable with the next generation through *The Mighty Mountain* children's picture book, perfect for family reading, Sunday school, or gifting to the young ones in your life.

- ❖ **The Study Guide**
  For readers who want the complete experience, *The Mighty Mountain: When the Ground Beneath You Shifts Study Guide* brings together the adult version, the children's story, and additional reflections, a resource designed for families, churches, and small groups.

- ❖ **Stay Connected**
  Sign up for updates, author news, and future releases so you never miss the next story designed to encourage and equip.

Your story matters. Keep climbing.

The Mighty Mountain (Children's Book Series)

"Even when the ground shakes, God's plan never wavers."

-A beautifully illustrated story that helps children see that every challenge is part of something mighty.

When the mountain begins to tremble, young readers journey with the characters to discover that sometimes what feels like a shake is really **growth, courage, and purpose unfolding**. Through vivid illustrations and gentle faith lessons, *The Mighty Mountain* helps children:

- Find comfort when life feels uncertain
- Learn that strength comes from God
- Discover the power of hope, community, and prayer

Perfect for ages **5–10**, this timeless parable opens conversations about **change, resilience, and trust in God's plan** — for families, classrooms, and Sunday school groups.

"A story that turns fear into faith — my kids still talk about it after bedtime."
— *Parent Reviewer*

"Beautifully written and deeply comforting for children navigating big emotions."
— *Educator, Fort Worth ISD*

Edition Type	ISBN
Hardcover	978-1-7362869-44-4
Paperback	978-1-7362869-51-2
eBook	978-1-7362869-37-7

(Available wherever books are sold — or at blkpawnpublishing.com)